Cromwell's Head

To Libby
in memory of absent
friends

**Cromwell's
Head**

Jim Greenhalf

**SMOKE
STACK
BOOKS**

best wishes,

Jim
4/8/23

Smokestack Books
1 Lake Terrace,
Grewelthorpe,
Ripon HG4 3BU

e-mail: info@smokestack-books.co.uk

www.smokestack-books.co.uk

ISBN 9781739173074

Smokestack Books
is represented by
Inpress Ltd

'There's a line of shadow on the far horizon
It could be stormclouds and it could be mountains...'

New Model Army

'Health and a modicum of wealth are all
I ask, dear Lord! That's surely not too tall
an order, is it? Just a few more years
to enjoy the status quo – before the tears.'

Nicholas Bielby, 'After Heine's Prayer'

Contents

Imperial Exodus

Did you see it, the last boat leaving?
Thank God they've gone. Good riddance.
All those years they've been telling us
what to do and how they want it done.
Things can only get better now, they say.
No more Pax this and Pax that.
When was the last time we did anything
out of order? That's what they've done to us.
The light will be purer now that its gleam
is unsullied by blood and eagles in their arenas.
And they call us barbarians!
They treated us like refugees in our own country:
changing our habits, our customs, words;
taking our women, thrusting themselves at us
like belly-piercing swords.
We paid for their empire, did their dirty work,
served as auxiliaries, while they tossed off
in their hillside summer villas.
Why did we let them do it for so long?

II

Well that's that, then. Four centuries
of empire in our wake. Down the hole.
I'm sorry to be going back.
Nothing glorious in that old ruin
of slaves and foreigners,
pouring like water across our borders.

Were we too dependent on them
to keep our way of life in order?
They said they were serving us,
but weren't they also serving themselves?
They knew we hadn't the money
to pay for our armies at home and abroad.

Fiddling, corruption, laziness, cowardice:
did we civilise the world for this?
We, who stand on the shoulders of
indomitable men of steel and marble?
I'll piss in the cup and pour a libation
on the head of any fat pontificating fool,

beating out the rhythm of our decline
like some mad *hortator*, dragging us back
to that bargain basement of fools and whores.
They won't survive; without us to protect them
they'll be eaten alive by jackals and wolves.
Too late for warnings. Do you think we'll be missed?

Indian Summer

Compared to this place
the river city of Benares
is a good place to die,
out of season,
the Ganges in flood.
And it's cheaper.

All that's required is:
seven hundred pounds of wood,
river water, incense,
a piece of white cloth,
a few mourners
and a boy with a stick
to rake the ashes
and crack open the skull
like a walnut.

It's been stella evening,
up here on the balcony,
sun going down over the river.
Wish we'd done it sooner.
Tusker and poor old Lucy
thought life would be
gin & tonics and toddy

on the veranda forever.
We didn't think the effort
would be worth the tuna
in the sandwich –
if you get my meaning.

True, I've made a bit of bunce
although my ships didn't all
come in; I kept going,
and eventually made my way –
once I'd got shot of you know what.

So much easier over there.
Vultures and dogs,
and anything in the river
with teeth and claws,
ensure that nothing
goes to waste
or rots.

No, I'm not a man of leisure.
What I do you wouldn't call it work –
work's become a dirty word –
I prefer rewarded pleasure,
extended play.

Boris Dancing

One step forward
  two steps back
dance in a rainbow
  clap, clap, clap.

Grin like a monkey
  flash like a Jack
two steps forward
  one step back.

All for one
  but better for some
wave those flags
  and sugar that plum.

Here comes dad
  but there goes mum
slap those sticks
  and bang that drum.

Everything is white
  then everything is black
turn those cheeks
  and give them a crack.

Down comes the hammer
  in go the nails
deliver us from evil
  in time for the sales

The Arrival

The men in black with peaked caps
at Huddersfield railway station,
stared at me: I glanced at them;
but they were not after me for crimes
against English literature:
they were awaiting the Prime Minister,
on a flying dutchman visit to the Powerhouse.

A blue and white Trans-Pennine Express
from Manchester slid into platform one.
Suddenly there he was,
the ship's captain-comedian.
Those slouching shoulders,
that flaxen bearskin of hair
on the collar, the men in black,
saluting people he passed
on his way to the exit.

Outside on the station piazza
Harold Wilson turned his back.
The old Pacer, taking me to Bradford,
laboured into evening's ill-lit gloom,
coughing like a Bronte.
Christmas was coming with an empty sack.

18 November 2021

Breaking the Circle

As the last US Sea King rises above Saigon,
again; as bulletins ricochet
and the old newsreels are re-run –
jet planes crashing in,
topless towers imploding;
brown shirts, black shirts,
on the march –
are the last days of Pompeii
really here
again?

Aristotle told world-conquering Alexander:
beware of history repeating itself.
First as tragedy then as farce,
Karl Marx or Brian Rix
added two thousand years later.

Having survived the news of wars, wars, wars –
Ulster, Iraq and Afghanistan –
am I, are we, any wiser?
We are mostly in the dark, drip-fed
by plasma screens
the size of football pitches
as, once again, farce bleeds into tragedy.

Things Fall Apart (for Some)

Sick or too sure of themselves,
men kill and die for something they cannot see:
some old Deuteronomy or sharia,
deaf and blind to reason.

Conflict, broken by the occasional tribal truce,
defines what began with water and wine.
Everything familiar to me is bombed,
news-flashed, trashed or silenced.

What used to be a mystery
of incense, ritual and ermine,
goes under the red wheel of history,
beaten into a fate only a few determine,

cancelling the idea of redemption.
And now everything seems either a miscarriage
or a mis-marriage. Promises are threats
or opportunities for a kind of treason.

Five Quintets

Right.
I've put up the house for sale,
knocked down the kennels
to a passing dog
and burned all the washing.

I've given away the copper
from your bottom drawer
and soldered the silver.
A man sleeping rough by the bus stop
got the keys to the camper.

I've donated the holiday home
to an order of small Bradford monks.
His letters are at the tip,
your knick-knacks are in the bin,
the cat is out and the taps are on.

In spite of the weather,
there's more to love
than a roll in the hay,
a dance round the pole or
farting through silk and leather.

So goodbye, good luck,
if your lucky number comes up.
No need for blame or truth –
once you've paid your solicitor
and the parting is absolute.

Everydog

In spite of never being asked to appear
on *Newsnight*, *The One Show* or *Strictly Come Dancing*,
I hear that an international poetry agency
with a data-base and algorithms,
is probing my background to see if I ever said anything
    interesting,
controversial or, God forbid, offensive, about anybody.

If fortune should ever thrust celebrity upon me
while I still have teeth, I have no interest in saying
'Wow!', 'Awesome!' or 'Iconic', on national TV;
nor in exploring my antecedents with Davina McCall.
If siblings are in hiding here, there or anywhere,
keep it that way. I don't wish them well.

I do not yearn to save humanity or rescue the planet,
and I'm not on a journey. When my time is done, I hope to go
into that good night without too much whining.
We are mostly mongrels trying to escape the kennel
and avoid the fate of refugees, washed up like seaweed on
    Dover beach.
Not every dog has its day in the sun.

If Only...

In memory of Bridget Baker, 1948–2023

We cannot avoid the past,
we cannot escape the consequences
of history. Maybe not,
but we can dream.

That night when Joseph Djugashvili
went down to the river
at Wapping with Litvinov
looking for women,
proved a red rag to Irish dockers
who punched him in the gob
severely;
but O, O, O, O, if only
Jim Connell's boys
had finished the job,

Flats above a Tesco Express
now mark the spot
where, in 1907,
history stopped,
briefly,
at a Quaker Chapel –
though not for God.

Better a Fool than a Monster

Does all the murdering maiming us daily
signify a world that's gone to the devil?
After all, Goodwood continues,
the towers of Ripon Cathedral still stand,
lifeboats and air-sea rescue risk life to save it.

With or without God,
death does not go unopposed.
We say, better the devil you know;
but what if death, famine, pestilence and war
are the only things you know?

Better a fool than a monster with a vision.
Prospero's brave new world of cloud-capped towers
and gorgeous palaces is best left to Disney –
not a brownfield site on the road to Damascus.

Armistice Sunday

Roads are being cordoned off with cones.
Around local war memorials men in high-vis bibs
arrange municipal chairs,
in readiness for the traditional fibs.
On the grid of a car-park where council offices
used to be, portable cabins raised on blocks
are staffed by masked recruits in blue.

They offer life-enhancing shots to my lucky generation
which escaped conscription when the law
was changed and we were freed
from the compulsion of compliance.
I see the young gathering again, arranged by uniform
in ranks. The discipline of doing this
gives them shape and purpose, I suppose.
I lasted a day in the Boys' Brigade.

The Queen cannot manage the Cenotaph this year.
Next year, or sooner, the wreath may be hers,
as the nation, collectively, bids goodbye
or good riddance, to the second Elizabethan era.
Big guns will salute her passing into history,
as they announced her entry in 1953.
When she's gone, I fear, we'll all be charlies.

November 2021

Wednesday, 31 January 1649

Tuesday, monarchy ends on the block.
The day after, business as usual –
the real shock. Everything going on
as it did before two that cold afternoon
when they stopped the clock.
The King's head was sewn back on,
the thread tied in a Windsor knot.

Nature appoints the wise to govern
the foolish, Milton wrote.
But what's the news when nature
loses its head, and fools
are empowered to rule instead?

Cromwell's Head

It took eight blows of the Tyburn axe
to separate Oliver Cromwell's head
from the body that carried it
through Civil War and England's
first and only Republic.

Impaled on a twenty-foot pike
outside Westminster Hall
for all the years of the cocker-spaniel
Parliament, as though a monstrous shrike
had fed on the Lord Protector:

plucking his eyes, then picking his brain,
as successive heads of state
rolled into Westminster and out again.
Bought and sold, passed around,
for three hundred years Cromwell's

eyeless head stared impassively
as the battles he fought and won
had to be fought all over again.
Until the ground we stand upon
was ceded, surrendered or given away

by fools, self-seekers and worse
whom he had driven out of Parliament.
A Bible and sword his ball and sceptre.
In the reign of Elizabeth Windsor,
Cromwell's head went underground;

but still it watches all that's done
in the headless people's name.
At a time unordered by rhyme or reason.
Call Andrew Marvell from his garden
to compose another ode for Cromwell's pardon.

Dark Times

The young do not have a past,
the old do not have a future.
So the young dream
and the old remember,
but cannot connect.

March on, march on:
the senile led by the infantile.
The higher-ups go 'Wheeeeeeee!'
in the front seat of the roller-coaster.
The rest are on speed or tranquillisers,
meeting ends they did not expect.

Dark times, dark times.
'What good can come of this?'
snapped jesting Pilate,
rucking back his sleeves to wash
as those around him clapped.

From a Metropolitan Police Launch

The world we look back upon:
who really knows the way it was?
The laws are no longer what they were
when this boat was launched,
between the wars.

What did water's lull-less lapping
mean to Anne Boleyn and Thomas More
as they were sculled
towards the maw
of Traitors' Gate?

How do we count the days
when they are circumscribed:
one day more,
or one day less?

One by one they slip
under the door
unnoticed –
until others run out of them.

Bring Back The Filthy Christians

In the bar of The Fighting Cock
a solitary man in red basketball boots,
denims, hair halfway down his leather back,
slumped, as though in mourning
for a band of brothers – *The Sinister
Cleaners*, perhaps.

The girl with the electric blues guitar,
whom I had come to interview,
was unborn when the Cleaners were partying,
as though tomorrow would never clock on.
But what did she know of true love?
The sad bastard at the bar ordered a double Jack.

Bring back *The Filthy Christians*!
his defeated demeanour seemed to scream.
Arrayed around the brown and cream interior,
dusty old jugs, alcohol-preserved dreams
of mad axemen who lost their bottle, their mojo,
their tomorrows; going off at half-cock.

A Vision of Judgement at Lunchtime

Unlike Lord Byron,
I am not given to visions;
but one lunchtime, I swear I saw
Sir Thomas More in heaven.

Contrary to his hair-shirt theology,
the old heretic-burner
had been told to dance a madcap Volta
to the Bee Gees *Staying Alive.*

'It will do him good!'
said the DJ, William Tyndale,
jabbing the air like John Travolta.
Sir Thomas danced without a hat.

Faces of Eternity

When Kathe Kollwitz
crawled out of the cratered centre
of the twentieth century,
what light other than black
did she have to draw the future?

Without hope, without fear:
but it's not Carravagio
swirling up out of the blackness;
nor Goya's carnival of freaks,
leering at the madness.

It's the scared face of the Man
in the Golden Helmet,
a face staring out at me from the wall
of my junior school,
a face that knew the Almighty

is neither Father Christmas
nor Torquemada and that triumph
is followed by disaster.
Why does he, why do they,
shadowy faces out of blackness

and silence, stare at me
as though I am a ghost?
Damnation, salvation:
we don't believe in either.
There's equality of a kind in that;

but still I apprehend
a before and after,
in spite of the plague of complicity
that locked up Irina Ratushinskaya,
for believing in a future

unplanned by Politbureau or Central Committee.
She spoke of this plague:
'We shall hold it back with our selves.
don't be afraid
on the other side of the world.'

But I am.

Storm from Heaven

for Michael Stewart

A summer storm
over Market Street, Thornton,
opened its fist,
wetting the people
crowding to watch you
speak from the front of the house
where the three sisters
were born.

Its suddenness,
that Friday evening,
felt like an augury
sent by Anne or Emily
to warn of something
yet to be lived.
A warning,
cursed or blessed?

The woman
from the museum
beside you,
sharing the shelter
of a red umbrella
the size of a bat's wing.
It failed to stop
the pelting weather
blowing everything inside out.

What good's an umbrella
under a storm from heaven?

Rocks

Simon Peter, whom Christ called 'The Rock',
denied his master thrice.

He swapped his rock
for a hard place; leaving
family, home and friends,
a loved and familiar place,
for what? The hope
of finding fire again;
if not the end, a beginning?

When I was younger,
lives were blocks of stone:
weathered, unchanging,
stable, withstanding
wind, rain, storms, adversity,
wild changes of affection.
Love sent me North.

Looking for redemption?
Look a bit further.
The white cliffs of Yorkshire
are not where they used to be.
Flamborough Head's
gone west
to Morecambe Bay.
Kilnsea, Ravenser Odd,
Ravenspur, Owthorne

and Hornsea Beck –
once sanctuary and shelter –
now under water,
pounded to pebbles and sand
for children's castles.

That line on the horizon,
is it a reclining Henry Moore,
or a silhouette of ruins
on England's edge?
A place where promises
were made and pledges kept
on pain of shame, exclusion, death.

She made her vows
and changed her name.
The sea washed away
a wedding bouquet.
The man rolling among
sea-weed and bladder-wrack
was not Michael Caine

but me.
In the smoke-filled days
of broadsheet news,
after I left Newcastle for good –
fifteen different addresses,
fifteen towns and cities –
I learned another kind of fiction.

Seeking shelter, sanctuary,
cresting the place of thorns
where the Brontes were born,
swapping a hard place
for a rock; for two decades,
until that summer of change.
Too restless to settle.

Rocks erode.
Lives are chalk
and then they're rain.

The Great Road North

When the Romans abandoned Britain
in the fifth century AD,
instead of the highway
they took to the water, leaving
the great road North for me.

On the magic bus from Victoria,
waiting for Scotch Corner –
my South-North border.
One day I would cross it for good,
but not like a cheque or postal-order.

On the road from Ripon
to Berwick, the rust-red
Angel of the North,
peering benignly over trees,
seemed to smile at me.

I could have been a hungry,
jobless squaddie
with bad memories
of The Shankill and The Falls;
blue and thin in a cracked house

on a Wallsend estate,
a skyline of rusting cranes
and silent winding wheels
rising to greet me every morning;
but I wasn't.

Finding Yourself

for Lesley

Glen Afric moon
silking cold blue lochs;
the dam your father built
at rainy Fasnakyle;
the narrow track upwards
that slips underfoot;
the sky's wet camber,
a glissando of rocks.

Up there, in that
rocky wilderness,
the empire of eagles,
beyond the reach
of man-made gods,
you either find or lose
yourself, whatever
the dreams that
trouble your sleep.

Fish out of Water

The Black Isle, low-lying
along the rim of the Moray Firth,
can be mistaken for cloud –
unless you're looking out to sea
from higher ground.
In war and peace your point of view
depends on how high up you are,
as legless Douglas Bader knew.

According to local legend
the four-pound salmon
encased above the exit of
Findhorn's beachside café,
was landed by the 'Squadron Leader'
in the summer of Thirty-seven.
But Bader, a fish out of water,
wasn't an RAF pilot then.

All that he wished for
came later. He flew against
the current of opinion,
spitting invective and bullets.
Four years trying to escape
from German display cases like Colditz
was fun. Defeat for him
came after the war was won.

Harriers

Tornadoes in three-of-spades
ripped the sky's blue zip-pasture,
making a jet-stream of thunder
above our rented Scottish bunker.

Could the pilots, banking over water,
spy the black harriers, crows
looking out from nests
in swaying, distant trees?

They never failed to see
the heaps of broken bread.
scattered in the garden,
unless they guessed

from quicker movements
of herring gulls and swifts,
flicking by like arrow-heads,
far too slick for me.

They glided in, spreading
Dracula wings over
unsuspecting dunnocks,
piking everything.

What they could not swallow
they stored under the wall
or the garden shed.
Gulls took off for roof-ridges

yellow beaks squawking
an air attack warning.
Starlings fled.
Fatter pigeons stayed put:

they'd seen all this before –
Flodden, Fyfe, Bannockburn, Culloden –
the bouncing, pigeon-toed strutting,
easy pickings among mounds of dead.

A Tricksy Feller

Didn't you seriously smell a rat
when he kept saying,
'My case comes up next Thursday'
on television?
Teasing, tantalising, confessing
almost; legally pursuing those
who got too close.
That batty *Back to the Future* hair,
Churchillian cigar, harlequin clothes,
disguising who he was and what he was doing
in all those dressing-rooms, hospitals.
Shaking hands with Elvis,
the Pope, confidante of prime ministers,
royalty, West Yorkshire Police,
the church.
More than a photo opportunity:
a guarantee, almost,
of authenticity.

No, I didn't.
I wanted to believe
his charisma and altruism were true,
like almost everybody
mesmerised by his speciality,
the common touch.

'If you're clever
you might make a mistake;
but I'm not clever:
I'm a tricksy feller.'
I saw the delight
in his eyes,
not the narcissism.

For fifty, sixty years,
balancing the lives he enhanced
against the lives he defiled.
Revelling in how
he had fooled the nation
with bling.

Seeing Me is Never Lovely

Seeing me,
in or out of print,
is never 'lovely'.
I'd be mortified if it was
the *Dance of the Sugar Plum Fairy*.

Probably it's just me,
out of 'wow'
with this selfie world,
where standing up for things
means bow-wow-wowing

in unison or kneeling down.
Used to be the other way round.
There is water in my well;
but it's cold
and hard to reach.

Look, let's face it,
I do not have the knack
Walt Whitman had
of making ordinary life
enjoyable.

But when the nurse
wiring up my ECG told me: 'Relax,
think of a beach.'
And I replied: 'How about Dunkirk, 1940?'
She laughed.

If genius really is one percent inspiration
and ninety-nine percent
perspiration, well,
I was always a big sweater –
never a big girl's blouse.

For Pete's Sake

In memory of Pete Cushway, graphic artist, husband, father,
artisan and nice old boozer

Every woman was darlin' to him,
including the one who married him
he stayed married to for fifty years.
'Back off man!' he once told her.

In Sixties' London he made a killing,
commercial drawing for a living.
A clever but unassuming man.
I liked him well enough.

'Can I have another beer?' was his mantra.
Opening another bottle or tin he'd say,
'Do you remember...' like a postman
inquiring his way.

I remember the day four of us
poled the hot streets of Dublin,
Temple Bar along the line of the Liffey,
to the Guinness factory at St James' Gate.

Not finding what we were looking for,
we had a beer instead.
A Jarvey rode us back in time
for the rush-hour dart to Skerries.

Mornings were fresh at the White Hotel,
fresh and blue beyond the tidal pull
to America. White pumps, slacks,
a scrubbed blue denim shirt

outside his pants,
cropped, white-bearded chin
jutting like a prow over rocks –
an old hippy boat captain.

He drew my portrait,
crafted a couple of pens,
turned chess pieces on the lathe in his shed;
but didn't judge people as pawns or kings;

thought they mostly muddled through like him.
I thought he'd be here long after me.
But he's taken a course
we cannot follow,

drawing away from his wake –
where we are now.
Back off Death!'
he would have said;

but Death had one empty
picture-frame left.

What Difference Does It Make?

Poetry's something to do between shows on the telly.
The social conditions in which it's written
have changed out of all recognition from the post-war
years of the Marshall Plan, before the old working
class ethic of self-help became an *I'm Alright Jack* joke.
Faber & Faber published Ted Hughes' *Hawk in the Rain*
in 1957 and Yorkshire's poetic Freddie Trueman
posed with Eliot, MacNeice and Auden holding sherry,
followed in 1966 by Heaney's *Death of a Naturalist*,
the year after Eliot popped his clogs. Poetry and pop music came
together in an orgy of unrepressed expression.
Those were the days; but then I was too young,
and now I'm too old for what has become
a self-regarding country hounded by trolls and dogs.

This is barely a country for men, young or old, Mr Yeats,
now that gender's negotiable and all is selfies
and reputations are undone by un-attributable blogs.
Oh come on all ye faithful, there's scarcely a dozen
poets in Western Europe, able to change the language
of a country's literary culture the way Dante did
and James Augustine Joyce attempted to.
Even Eliot, who gonged the Nobel Prize for Poetry
nearly half-a-century before famous Heaney,
described himself as 'minor' compared to Shakespeare, Donne
and Dante Aligheri. Would-be writers should
firstly learn their craft, like Michelangelo did
in the quarries of Cararra, or welders who dream of
turning base metal into ocean-going liners.

If you really are a poet shouldn't you be able
to recite by heart and, better still, improvise a theme
the way that Miles Davis or Beethoven could

on trumpet and keyboard (a Broadwood).
I used to recite by heart, like all young children
are expected to in parts of Europe; but only when
someone else wanted it; I needed another's ears
to hear myself. That seems like ancient history now –
a few bits of discarded amphora a retreating army
leaves behind in a desert storm. Not *Ozymandias*
exactly; but then I don't consider myself a poet
the way that people think of Virgil or Tony Harrison.
I use a few simple poetic techniques – assonance,
rhythm, occasionally rhyme – to tell my stories.

No, I am not James Fenton, nor was meant to be;
just a former provincial newspaper reporter
who's been known to write the news in *terza rima*.
In a weekly column I sometimes wrote verse satires
of a political nature: a piece on Margaret Thatcher
returning in triumph from the Falklands,
in the style of marvellous Andrew's Horation Ode
to Britain's first dictator, Oliver Cromwell.
In the 'Loadsamoney' gloom of Nigel Lawson's
budget – was this the *Jerusalem* of William Blake
– I had an entire poem on the features page,
juxtaposing that benighted age with the life
and values of Bradford-born Fabian J B Priestley,
headlined *Out of Passion with the Times.*

Now I'm out of fashion too, along with Andy Croft,
poet-publisher of this book, and dear old David Tipton,
poet, novelist, translator and editor of *Redbeck Press*,
who did more for the world's unacknowledged
legislators than Percy Bysse and Lord George Gordon.
But life's a bust and all good poets, like prime ministers,
must come to dust. Even Elvis ran out of sand
in the hotels of Las Vegas, so why not you or me?
Though I'm too old for sex and impro-poetry

of the sort celebrated in the *The White Hotel*,
by the other doubting Thomas – Donald Michael –
I've had my moments in Bradford, London,
Manchester and Prague and though my dog's
not laughing as it used to do, I've earned a crust.

These days my preference is for silence,
not the sound of music either by Wolfgang Amadeus
or that other Van the Man – Beethoven.
If you think that poetry is more or less the same
as stand-up, it's Michael McIntyre whom you want
to hire or, better still, Boris dancing Johnson,
who's not ashamed to spray his audience with
fake champagne. For those who miss Roger McGough
doing *Poetry Please* – my poems didn't strike a chord
apparently, nor, I imagine, did those of Mr Croft –
let me confess: I was raised on rhyming couplets
performed by Cyril Fletcher on *Workers'Playtime*.
Resurrected on BBC1 on Sunday nights
to raise a laugh for Esther Rantzen's *That's Life*.

But what does poetry mean and who is it for?
Would it speak to Alan in Sally Wainwright's *Last Tango in
Halifax* or stuck-up Celia in boring Harrogate?
What difference does it make for Abraham or Sally
serving, say, with Médicins Sans Frontières?
Although Mr W H (Auden) once likened poetry
to a flickering flame in solitary lamps,
what would Howard, Marina or Pearl
in Roy Clarke's *Last of the Summer Wine*
make of the image? Would it strike a hopeful light
for folk in darkness queuing outside food banks
between Ripponden and the Isle of Wight?
Food for the soul's important:
I don't suppose that well-off Alan and Celia
live by bread or tinned baked beans alone,

or even capppucino with a cinnamon swirl.
Words in their own way can be fulfilling
as the steak and kidney pudding dinners
dished up, I hope, at Thirsk's Old Red House.
It's how they're organised before they're served.
These days even poetry needs validating,
especially in Britain's universities,
those bastions of intellectual bravery.
Remember little Jess in Jeanette Winterson's
Oranges Aren't the Only Fruit running
joyfully through the streets of Accrington
shouting, 'I'm going to Oxford!'
Now it seems poetry needs a cultural visa
to breathe the same air as Howard, Pearl and Marina.

Quo Vadis. The end is nigh for those who've come this far –
notice I refrained from 'navigate', 'journey' and vision
ditto 'harshen my mellow' – a New York decorator
on *Interior Design Masters* recently.
My God, I am truly a man behind the times.
Mine began when bolshie Robert Bolt was writing
A Man for all Seasons and I dribbled a ball across
Tottenham's acrid marshes to watch Spurs do the League
and FA Cup double; that changing time when football
was poetry in motion with a soundtrack to match;
a time of Barenboim and Jacqueline du Pré.
Before I swap the telly for the other box, or slip
into landfill in Devon, here's my plea: some kind soul
ring a bell for poetry – the bread and fish of heaven.

Don't Let Facts Spoil a Good Story

Don't lean against the bar
like a superannuated Alun Weaver
and, drink in hand, regale us with tales about
Dylan Thomas and Richard Burton
carousing in Welsh wartime coastal towns
of casual liaisons.

And how they prowled the bars of Newquay's
Black Lion hotel and, down the shoulder
of the tilting hill, raised hell in the Bluebelle,
huddled in its wallflower corner
above the harbour.

How the cherubic poet-reporter and pock-faced actor
knocked the bolts out of boiler-makers,
making brassy tills jingle and brassier women
tingle with the hope of sex and money
on wartime Friday nights.

I've heard the one about the Special Forces soldier,
paddling across the blacked-out, big-mouthed bay,
spraying Sten gun bullets
across the White House ceiling,
all because the rumour that his wife and Thomas
had a Friday feeling.

Tell me instead about the two hundred broadcasts
he scripted for the BBC, word perfect, on time;
and the work he did with Eliot, Arlott and Auden.

I don't want to hear, yet again,
about the eighteen shots of Scotch
that no-good boyo is supposed
to have downed in New York's
White Horse Tavern.

Dead poets, like dead singers, may be a tonic;
but what's the story of another
sad-sack poet's pitiful death
really worth in an age
when talent's less entertaining
than excess?

Anthology

At first it was like meeting old friends
on a long train of many memories.
Such promiscuity made a change:
all the loving and unloved,
the sad, self-loving and unlovely,
in close proximity between the sheets.

I did not expect the company of Brecht
and Mayakovsky, McMillan and Berger:
citizens of an old republic of poetry
heading home from a foreign country,
or going back to a foreign country;
their only visa their poetry.

But after a week or two
the mass of it felt oppressive.
The dull reality of meaning
little or nothing to each other
was like being buried alive,
under a landslide, a mountain.

Going Back

Some people want to believe
that lizards or loonies really have taken over.
True or not, the buck
never stops.
When truth is bashed about like a puck,
better check the country's flux capacitor.

As in the days of Henry VIII,
guilt is presumed.
Innocence is a state that must be proved,
after Africa and India.
Better break out those lavender loons
of men behaving sadly
in the Seventies.
Better remove the old screwed-up balls
of News of the World
from those platform shoes
and step out.

If the state is tottering,
nobody will notice you
tottering too.

Call Me Isabelle

Now that history's being abolished
like accountability and reasonable doubt,
what is it you want me
to worry about?

Like everyone older than Sizewell 'B',
I am running out of energy.
Only the other night I dropped off
during *Match of the Day*.

When I woke,
Chelsea were three down
to Leeds United.
And I'd missed all of them.

Just like Germans
and the Treaty of Versailles,
we too have bad memories
of penalties.

Call me sentimental.
Call me rebarbative.
Call me Isabelle
if it makes you feel any better.

You speak your truth
and I'll speak mine;
that way both of us will be
in two minds.

What counts, it seems,
is not what you do,
but what you say you did
and who you say it to.

Nowadays, it pays
to be immersive,
inclusive and global,
not subversive.

Cranks turns on chance
events, ignorance and ideals.
From which end of the bridge
over troubled waters

is next mad bastard coming?

In God's Acre

Sara Clarke: a feisty friend
25/3/1937–29/6/2022

Looking up from the valley,
the red pantiled roof of her house,
detached from its neighbours,
stands out like a fiery warning.
Twenty-two years she lived in it,
dispensing gruff, no-nonsense
kindness; flying the White Rose
above her independence.

But not this morning.
Looking down into her slot,
the Moravian Church behind,
dust from my handful of earth
catches a passing breeze
as it drops, pattering like grain
on the top of her studded
biodegradable box.

A gnarled root,
a twisted prophetic finger,
cut off from a dead
patriarchal Hawthorn, sticks out.
She was a thorn in my side
until Pashley died.
She was with him at the end.
I'd go to see her then.

'I don't tell people what to do!
Why are you laughing?'
Her cheeks, two Fred Dibner furnaces,
glowed like October apples.
She buzzed like the bees she kept,
made life about her bloom,
put its worth into overalls
and set it to work for others.

Now she's busy underground.
And here am I looking down,
but to what purpose?
The White Rose at half-mast,
her Mount of Olives garden,
all gone. Hard to imagine.
Paradise under the hammer,
at half-a-million.

Under the Eyes of Eagles

for John and Alice Spurr

I

I've got a friend I've never seen.
He lives the life of Jeremiah Johnson,
with his wife in a cabin they built
above Lake Tagish in the Yukon.
They share forests with elk and caribou,
brown bears, black wolves;
and walk on water when it's frozen.
Lopping logs, splitting them,
cook-wood and kindling;
they take trout from the lake
and water for drinking, washing,
cleaning. For stores and mail
they motor-boat and snow-mobile
to Whitehorse. Every morning
they repair and stake out trails,
so they know where they're going
when mists twist into fog
that hangs from the branches of
torchwood fir and pine.
Fifty years they have lived this way.
They used to winter in California.
Now they prefer the extremes
of white and green,
under the eyes of eagles;
at peace, mostly.

II

From a Wildfire Service airtanker,
it looks like paradise –
the clear water of the lake,
the never-ending treeline beyond.
But the *Whitehorse Daily Star*
crackles with incendiary opinions.
The city, they say, is going
up in smoke or down the drain.
Opiods and booze; the feckless
and reckless down on 4th
and Alexander; and
regional political correctness.
It seems that everyone
has some kind of pain
they are trying
to dowse or inflame.
You don't have to go
north to Alaska
to find a wilderness.

Donkeys and Ponies

Shabash little donkey.
For you the road never ends,
carrying the burdens of others.
Only when your will is worn down
to a hoof, a blunted Khyber top,
does your heart give up the holy ghost
and stop. Until then,
shabash little donkey,
tied to the burden of others,
until you drop.

Get along gentle fell pony,
Lakeland sunshine in your eyes;
your muscles made this landscape.
Now your strength and endurance
are surplus to requirement.
You trusted us: we cut you off,
balancing your death
against retirement's cost.
The masters
miss their servants now.

The Last Monarch

In the last days of summer,
the afternoon of your departure,
I was on the Paddington train
from Oxford, watching a rainbow
trying to construct itself
above the wet fields of farms –
a week of rain after drought
had brought warnings of catastrophe.

I reached my destination.
not knowing you had gone.
The evening sun was out.
My first thought was trivial:
your milliner supplied you hats
better than Boy George's.

I saw your class act twice,
on Market Street, Centenary Square.
The royal Rolls or Bentley,
the twirling of the hand,
the retinue of dogs –
more tail-wagging than
Elizabeth Taylor knew.

If that represented Britishness
it was from an era beyond
Vaughan Williams, Elgar,
the annual Cenotaph morning,
World War Two,
and post-imperial arguments
about collective identity.

No man is an island,
of himself entire,
the words of John Donne
came out of the darkness.
They echoed in your voice.
'We will meet again', you said:
the first time I believed
your words represented you
and not a position.

Towards the end,
you became an old lady –
the hats began to slip
like a candle-snuffer,
the shepherd's crook of your back,
thickening ankles,
pursing painted lips,
a stick to lean upon.

Everything was defined
by the state you embodied.
It stumbles on like a queue,
as you fade into history
with the memory of
a late September afternoon,
a procession, a slow march,
massed bands, a bell and a drum.

Charlie's not my darling,
but I hope he's lucky and good.
I may not live to see
the crowning of William,
perhaps the last monarch
of the dis-United Kingdom.
After him, a factitious republic
squabbling over treaties
with fractious neighbours?

Your legacy depends on
how well new generations
feel bound to each other,
and whether old words
become new words
of opprobrium,
in the mouths of comedians.

30 September 2022

A King Speaks

If I am mad
let me be mad
in my own way.

If I am sad
let me be sad
in my own way.

But if I stand
in the tide
to prove a point

let me be wiser
than my sad, mad
followers who believe

a king of England,
Denmark and Norway,
can defy

the ministry of waves.

Coronation Express

Going up to the Wolds to paint the trees –
South Kensington to Bridlington –
David Hockney liked to listen to
Paul Temple crime thrillers.

So when we were locked down, shut in,
we too dropped the news for Francis Durbridge
repeats on BBC4 Extra – *Paul Temple
and the Jonathan Affair* from 1963.

A postcard from Harrogate, a gold signet ring,
Paul and wife Steve – Peter Coke (*say it Cook*)
and Marjorie Westbury – dashing
from one London address to another,

to Vivian Ellis' *Coronation Express*.
The plot, convoluted, the ending, inexplicable;
but where would I have been, growing up,
without Martyn C Webster and the BBC Drama Repertory?

Mock on, if you like; but Wilfred Pickles
and Jimmy Clitheroe put the North on the air
long before Ted Hughes' Calder consonants
cracked like rocks in my southern ear.

And later, Tony Warren's doom-scrolling
Ena Sharples, Martha Longhurst and Minnie Caldwell
superseded Shakespeare's witches, stirring things up
over stout, port and lemon, instead of a cauldron.

By the twitching of my thumbs,
something vexing this way comes,
tweeting, texting, day and night,
itching to set the bloody world to rights.

Think on!

Aliens in a City of Culture

I once shared a stage
with Wild Willi Beckett,
psycho-surgeon to the nation
and twice the Monster Raving Loony Party's
prospective Parliamentary candidate.
His poem that night – 'Capital of the Universe' –
imagines an Alien looking for heaven on earth.
It goes to Tokyo, Paris, Brasilia;
but settles for cosmopolitan Bradford.
Made perfect sense to me in September, 1997:
the city's Centenary,
the year that the Queen came,
John Major's Government went,
Tony Blair arrived
and Lady Diana died.

Actor-manager Barrie Rutter,
Creative Briton of the Year,
wanted to make Willi's wild idea pay
by staging a triple bill of Shakespeare plays
in Centenary Square. But time bleeds.
After nine years he took
Wars of the Roses to Leeds.
It was enough to turn the friendliest Alien
into one of those Tetley Bittermen
imagined by Stephen 'Seething' Wells.
So much for Priestley, Hockney,
Margaret McMillan and most of the Brontes;
and other free radicals, under whose skin
this place of chapels and hills,
valleys and mills, inked its imprint.

James Hill, Tony Richardson
and Simon Beaufoy
won four Oscars between them;
and yet this UNESCO City of Film
ditched its annual film festival.
You'd have to be from another planet,
like Wild Willi's Alpha Centaurean,
to get your heads round that idea.

Eight Americans at Carlo's, Alnwick

As the Coen brothers say before every film:
this is based on a true story

I thought they must be Americans,
the four women who trooped in –
they weren't wearing trainers.
The shoes of one of them
could have come from the front window
of Jobson's on Hotspur Street:
Dubarry's, for horse-chasers.

They came from Minnesota.
They'd left Minneapolis,
the Lake Superior Hills,
for Market Street, NE66, schooners
of fish, chips and hot gravy,
and shopping on Holy Island.

Was it Sterling's plunging value
against the sad old dollar?
Maybe they were a White House delegation,
on their way back from Berwick,
to see if the town on the Tweed
was still technically at war with Russia?

They asked where we were staying.
I told them Boulmer – say it "Boomer" –
with the FBI. They left in a hurry.
The Fishing Boat Inn, I could have told them.

Within minutes four more, two women, two men,
marched in. They wore identical masks
and hunkered down at the same neighbouring table.
One of them asked why we were staying
near an RAF station, and what did we know
about Berwick's latest situation?

Death in Soho

Randall Swingler 1909–1967: poet, journalist, publisher,
musician, playwright, novelist, communist, war-hero

Did they lull him to sleep
with *Desert Island Discs,*
Two Way Family Favourites,
and *Down Your Way*?
No, that was us.

His fate was different,
dropping dead in the streets
of Soho, on the town,
in the Summer of Love.
A grey, rumpled heap

like a screwed-up *News of the World*.
Not news now, the famous poet
whose words and music
brought thousands
to concert halls,

all across London;
before the war
his name and face
standard.
Were you there?

Drinking in
the sunny June air
of Shaftesbury Avenue,
when that LCC ambulance
took his life away?

His only audience that day:
a sweating policeman,
his weeping daughter,
and passers-by,
wondering whose life

was trickling away
like water,
the last notes of a song,
everything you cannot
put your finger on

that makes a difference.
I don't remember his name
on the news, his face
in the papers,
another forgotten war-hero

beached on a London street,
washed up,
on the floor you might say.
Given the choice
between love and hate,

people choose love,
don't they,
to bleed and suffocate?
He knew, of course;
but knowledge made no difference

to the trade
he chose to make.
It was more than a cause
greater than himself,
survival could not mitigate.

Long Hot Summers

In the after-gloom of the Summer of Love,
he rose like a dybbuk in the suit
of a Black Country mortician
and raised a crooky warning finger.

Unless something drastic was done
West Indian bus conductors and nurses,
South-east Asian doctors and shop-keepers,
would over-run the streets of London,
Solihull, Kingston-upon-Thames and Wolverhampton.
White blood and black blood would flow
and the waterways of England foam
like Ancient Rome's old man Tiber.
Had Windrush torpedoed the Empire?

And then that long hot summer of *I'm Not in Love*,
England's South African cricket captain declared:
'I intend with the help of a few others
to make the West Indies grovel.'
But under the umpire's crooky warning finger,
West Indies scorched England's bowling and batting.

The cricket brought relief for some.
The heat brought standpipes, rain dances,
a Black Country Minister of Drought:
Howell! Howell! Howell!

That summer our mettle was tempered
in fire and water and, as Derek Walcott said,
'the red ripeness of runs' – not blood.

From the Coffee Gallery, Bagshot

Yaseem, our local postmaster,
asked me how long *all this*
was likely to go on?
A lifetime at least, I told him.

We know the world leaves everyone behind:
you, me, the missing neighbourhood cat –
chipped and neutered; but the soul's self
goes somewhere else forever.

That's what *The Watchtower Bible and Tract
Society of New York* wants me to believe.
Invisible representatives left a rack
of pamphlets – 'Enjoy Life Forever!' –

under the railway station's old olive tree.
The cover picture shows a young man
walking towards storm-clouds or mountains
along a streak of lightning.

Evidently torrential rain may be expected
in paradise. Though my coffee's cold,
I'll drink to the thought of that.
Silent flashes of lightning last night,

and today rumbling downpours,
augured in our new Prime Minister.
Signs of warning or wonder
in days gone by.

I was inclined to hope so myself –
until I heard the lady speak.
Yaseem was unimpressed.
He thinks we don't have long.

If a judging god exists beyond the vanishing point
of the next event horizon,
will he or she or them or it be kind to us
like Monty Don?

3 September 2022

A Day at the Races

One of those titanic, Battle of Britain skies,
ice blue, vapour trails skating across it,
thirty-thousand feet above
black swallow-tail coats, toppers, summer frocks

and meringue hats tipping like landslides,
getting out of private taxis at Bagshot station
for a day at the races – Ascot
one stop down the track.

And as I watched – they nodding, smiling –
I saw them in the big ship's ballroom,
waiting for an invitation to the Captain's table,
an April night, the trip of a lifetime;

the women and their men, dressed
to defy the improbable, buoyed
by more self-confidence than the Mitfords.
And I thought that some believe

survival is a birth-right.
And I thought of top hats floating,
half-filled boats, lights going out
amid rafts of ice.

Autumn Statement

While one man eats
another man bleeds.
The wind in the barley,
the birds in the trees.
One man wants,
another man needs.

Love, O careless love
may be rare as the sight
of an articulate toucan,
a perfect gentle knight,
or lucky Lord Lucan
shooting the breeze,

but it's not a myth.
Though I'm following no-one,
I try to live for something.
But if I must die for nothing
let it be with my boots on,
not on my knees.

In the prism of these crazy days,
teach the little lamb to graze
the sunnier uplands of its home
lest others buy and sell it,
by tickertape or phone,
for compound fees.

Going nowhere? Go there fast,
before the present
overwhelms the past
and tragedy
turns into farce
that no-one sees.

Elegy for a Warrior of Light

Alone in Airedale,
waiting for a doctor to tell him
why his blood pressure was collapsing.
The sun sank so low that afternoon,
the hills westwards over the railway bridge
had no gold in them.

Hard to believe that he
was once a warrior of light.
Even during that terrible strike
he did not believe that fourteen pounds
of Kevlar body armour
were necessary to fight
the good fight.

Some nights I can see no farther
than the pot-holed tarmacadam
of the municipal car-park
where rain abandons its mirrors,
the moon's small wasteland
above decorated masonry.

Roughing it with the smooth,
raising another glass,
a congenial circle of blighted minds
smirking in public places –
is that the answer?

I never saw that in him,
even in fading light,
when I looked in the mirrors
left by the rain.

Soon they'll be lighting up the village again –
abstracts of the Nativity that won't offend,
prisms and wreaths of love and peace.
While at night black four-by-fours
slide silently by – on lease.

Fugitives

Seems like only yesterday
when we used to wait for
Ray Harryhausen to set in motion
unworldly gods and monsters,
to help or hinder Jason
and his crew of Argonauts
to make their big steal –
the Golden Fleece.

There are no gods now,
only monsters
trying to shear us like sheep.
There is no place of safety.
This is not a flying island
defying the gravity of nightmare.
The cross that we bear
is not a ladder to heaven.

It is not what we know as home.
Home is what we carry.
This place might as well be the Moon.
Above this dead man's zone
sits a peaceful-looking cloud,
unreachable as a Black Sea beach
or a sofa on the border.
Where do we go from here?

Like the dogs of Chernobyl,
we're turning feral:
self-reliant, cunning,
non-compliant.
We are the non-citizens
of a cashless habitat,
where only the wind moans.
A free state of bones.

Pay What You Like

Written specially for the 2022 Ripon Poetry Festival

Pay what you like for this poetry show.
Pay what you like for a labracadabra-doodle.
Pay what you like for a hybrid with circular vision.
Pay what you like to the devil you know.

Speaking of whom,
the Chancellor of the Exchequer,
sent me a letter.
It said: dear tax-payer,
without you
the country wouldn't be
what it is today.
Since you were laid off
and no longer pay as you earn,
pay what you like
either in money or kind.

Pay what you like for a ticket to ride.
Pay what you like to the BBC.
Pay what you like for a Sky Glass television.
Pay what you like for your heart or mind.

Affordable Cremations
sent me a recorded delivery.
It said: take as much time
as you need to die.
And when it's your turn,
we'll dispose of you
for next to nothing:
we call it 'pay as you burn'.

So pay what you like for a schloss on the Rhine.
Pay what you like to St Peter or St Paul.
Pay what you like for heaven on earth.
Pay what you like for peace in our time.

Back Off Death

Carl Jung, Face to Face with John Freeman in 1959, said:
'There is something in us that doesn't believe in death.'

Back off Death,
there are not many of us left.
Old dogs like me,
who've seen and heard a lot;
felt the shock-wave
and lost heart or nerve
more than once; who've been
gored or mocked in public
or, worse, ignored.

Back off Death,
although to say so baldly
is a waste of breath.
I'm tired of waking every morning
with you sitting inside me,
like unsolved murders or poison gas.
Aberfan, Enniskillen, Bradford City, Dunblane –
to you the senseless is all the same,
nothing personal.

Back off Death.
Don't think that, because
you're inevitable like rent and taxes,
the world's tenancies of flesh
belong exclusively to you, Herr Flick,
the bailiff of apocalypse.
Even Alfred Russel Wallace
believed that life goes on
beyond the Styx.

So back off Death,
ride back to the devil you know –
the landlord of the twentieth century,
who seems to own
the freehold of this one too.
This Everydog pledges to do his best.
While I still have heart,
the end of my nose
is where the frontline starts.

Postscript and Acknowledgements

'Imperial Exodus' I and 'II', and 'Everydog' were first published in 2022 in the Huddersfield University Grist anthology: *We're All in it Together: Poems for a Disunited Kingdom*. Writing for that book in August and September, 2021, prompted me to carry on and find this one. In the poem 'Indian Summer', an expat looks back. Tusker and Lucy are characters in Paul Scott's Booker Prize-winning novel *Staying On*. Trevor Howard and Celia Johnson played Tusker and Lucy Smalley in the film version of *Staying On*.

In 1907 Joseph Stalin, along with a lot of other revolutionaries whom he would later kill, attended the Fifth Congress of the Social Russian Democratic Party in Hackney, London, not far from where I used to share a basement flat. I discovered this coincidence only last year, which prompted the poem 'If Only...'

A slightly longer version of the final verse of 'Seeing Me is Never Lovely' first appeared in the Redbeck Press volume 'Blue on Blue' in 2005. The fictional name of Alun Weaver in 'Don't Let Facts Spoil a Good Story', belongs to Kingsley Amis' Booker Prize-winning novel *The Old Devils*. The unnamed 'Tricksy Feller' is the late Jimmy Savile. In 'What Difference Does it Make?' *Quo Vadis* – where are you going? – was a question put to Christ by Peter. In 1951 MGM made it into a film about how Christianity subverted the Roman Empire. 'Our new Prime Minister', in 'From the Coffee Gallery, Bagshot', was Liz Truss. The late Enoch Powell MP and cricketer Tony Grieg feature in 'Long Hot Summers'.

'Pay What You Like' was written for the final day of the 2022 Ripon Poetry Festival. A draft of 'The Last Monarch' was given an airing there and subsequently amended. Alfred Wallace Russel, in 'Back Off Death', was a pioneering evolutionist, a contemporary of Charles Darwin and Sir Arthur Conan Doyle, who came to believe that Evolution was only part of the world's story.

Thanks to Michael Stewart for causing all this in August, 2021, to Peter Snow for the front cover image and much criticism and encouragement along the way and to poet and painter Nicholas Bielby, for the lines in the front of this book. The late Peter Cushway drew the portrait on the back cover. Andy Croft should be given the chance to politely decline an MBE or OBE for keeping the aspidistra flying for writers generally and for giving this particular text the black light of printer's ink.

Lesley, my partner and companion, gave me time and space for all the visions and re-visions. Her son William supplied most of the copy-paper. Without these generous people and others – such as writer, poet and editor of 'The Interpreter's House' poetry magazine, Merryn Williams; Alan Dent, writer, poet and editor of The Penniless Press and the MQB poetry magazine; the late Sebastian Barker, poet and editor of The London Magazine; former Yorkshire Post features editor John Yates, and the late, extraordinary David Tipton, of Redbeck Press – I might have lost my head.